THE MILLENNIAL WAY

STEP UP • STEP OUT • STEP FORWARD

DECLAN WILSON

I0493152

TABLE OF CONTENTS

FOREWORD

Her engagement ring glistened in my hand.

As I stared at it, I wondered—"Do I really have what it takes to do this?"

Kate was (and is) way out of my league—a witty, gorgeous redhead with a tongue sharp as a tack and a glare that could crack ice. She can brighten a room or bring it to a thunderstorm in seconds. She is at once perceptive and empathetic. She expects your best, and has no trouble telling you when you haven't met it. Any given Saturday in the fall she will be drinking more beer than you, screaming "ROLL DAMN TIDE," and then flashing a beaming smile outlined by a constellation of freckles.

This is the woman I dreamed of marrying.

But it wasn't the proposal I was worried about. (Although I should have. Maybe I'll tell that story one day.)

I was worried about what would happen next.

So many Millennials are searching for a path. We know the world isn't what it was when our parents grew up, but the dust hasn't quite settled yet. We live in a world of suffocating possibility. All the barriers have broken down. We feel inadequate if we are not millionaires by 28.

Or 26.

Or 22.

What's the formula? Around every corner the headlines shout— "10 EASY LIFE HACKS" or "7 THINGS TO DO WITH YOUR MONEY TODAY!" At best this advice is general, blanket wisdom; at worst it's an advertisement.

We are plagued by questions:

Should we pursue higher education or do degrees even matter?

Should we get a "real job" or try and piece together freelance work?

Should we give up on our dream or risk it all as an entrepreneur?

And what about those of us with families? So what if there are people making a killing by living in their car and staying up all hours of the night? Do we have to give up on what we *want* most in order to make a decent living for those we *care about* most? What's the equation? What buttons do we push?

Declan gives us an answer to all these questions.

As the quintessential Millennial—26, tattooed, dreamer, he also comes equipped with a lot of real life "baggage"—a wife, a child, and a real job. The combination of these experiences is at once inspirational and practical. He won't tell you this, but he's one of the most patient and understanding people you'd ever meet. He's not in this for the money. If he were, you would have paid a lot more for this.

Read this book. Read the stories of those Declan has interviewed. Don't just look at what they've done, but *how* they've done it.

Does your path look like the woman who started something online and wound up at her dream job? Or is it the other way around, are you going to start in the unwashed masses and decide to Step Out instead?

I don't know. Declan doesn't know.

Everyone has a different path, and instead of prescribing a guarantee, Declan offers guidance, insight, and reflection from both his own story and those he's talked with.

Although it's called *"The Millennial Way,"* these chapters transcend the generational gap. The steps in the following pages can be used as a guideline for everyone from the 16-year-old graphic designer deciding whether or not she should go to college to the 59-year-old on the brink of retirement wondering what he should do next.

This book isn't a "fail-proof guide to success," and I know Declan wouldn't want it to be. We both know better than that because there's something I haven't told you yet:

There is no formula to success.

There is no equation for happiness.

There is only a mindset.

Welcome to The Millennial Way.

Todd Brison
toddbrison.com

INTRODUCTION

"Our youth now love luxury. They have bad manners, contempt for authority; they show disrespect for their elders and love chatter in place of exercise; they no longer rise when elders enter the room; they contradict their parents, chatter before company; gobble up their food and tyrannize their teachers."

Ah, the old adage about Millennials. When I hear quotes like the one above, I laugh because so many predictions about our generation by the early oracles never came true. Granted, the above quote did come from a reputable source. You may have heard of him.

His name is Socrates.

The notion that the younger generation is not as refined as their predecessors is a tale as old as time. In the late nineties, as Y2K loomed closer and closer, the idea of a new generation coming into fruition worried a lot of people. This new generation, aptly labeled "Millennial," would be the first generation to come of age in the new millennium. Early predictions about this new generation pegged them as entitled, lazy, narcissistic, and self-absorbed. Some even went on to rename them "Generation Me-Me-Me."

I am a Millennial, which may account for some of the bias in my writing, but the fact remains that this generation is far from the "gobbling" and "tyrannizing" Socrates so eloquently predicted. I'm not saying we're perfect; some individuals in our generation fit the typical stereotypes of being self-absorbed, lazy, and entitled. But what generation doesn't have their fair share of bums?

Many of the Millennials I encountered while researching this book don't ask themselves, "What can the world give to *me*?" Instead they ask, "What can *I* give to the world?" It's time people realize we are a generation poised to make a difference, primed to share our talents, and prepared to tackle the major issues previous generations failed to solve.

In this book, I will introduce an impressive collection of young individuals who disprove the selfish stereotypes. Granted, I can't make the claim that these selected individuals account for the entire Millennial generation. However, they represent a growing niche with a lot to offer, a niche with a dream-chasing formula that anyone can apply to their life, no matter how old they are.

MILLENNIAL FACTS

I want to first start this book with some basic facts about Millennials. For our sake, I am defining a Millennial as anyone born between the years of 1980 and 2000. However, those on the fringes of this arbitrary boundary can decide for themselves if they want to be included.

Millennials are an interesting bunch; we are more diverse than our generational counterparts, we're on track to become the most educated generation in history, and, at the time of this writing, we've entered a workforce facing the worst recession since the Great Depression (1929-39). However, those lucky enough to hold a job are no better off.

In a recent Pew Research Center study, less than a third of the Millennial respondents said they make enough money to live the life they want. And more than a third admitted to receiving financial help from their parents. So no, things haven't been great for us at the onset, but instead of complaining, we're doing something about it.

Unlike previous generations who worked their entire life at one job, Millennials are on the move, keeping a lookout for the next opportunity to present itself. According to a Pew Research Center 2010 report, "About two-thirds of all employed Millennials say it is 'very likely' or 'somewhat likely' they will switch careers sometime in their working life, compared with 55% of Gen Xers and 31% of Baby Boomers. Remarkably, nearly six-in-ten of employed Millennials say they already have switched careers at least once."

I'm one of the six-in-ten who have already changed jobs early in their career. Two years into a career I worked hard to establish, I made the switch. Why? I wasn't happy.

We can debate all we want whether or not job-hopping is the answer, but I think Millennials are on to something: if we don't like our current situation, we seek to improve it.

How to Read this Book
So what's the big deal here?

Sure, I can spew off some facts about Millennials I found on Google, slap them together in a Word Doc, publish it as a PDF and call it a day. But I didn't spend eight months interviewing Millennials to compile bar trivia. You see, I have this theory. I believe a path exists, a Millennial way per se, that few have forged on their way to a happy, healthy, and fulfilling life.

Why is it we see so many brave young people taking risks to chase dreams while we hold back, thinking our hopes are utterly crazy to pursue? Why would an English major take a break from college to spend time on a startup? What drives someone to leave their well-paying tech job to run an online coffee store? How does one pack up their life, move to a new city, and chase a dream of starting a music career?

I wanted answers, so I sought out those who could help me find them: Millennials doing awesome things with their lives. I wanted to discover what set them apart, what drove them, and what they are seeking. In other words, I wanted to learn *the way*.

So what is the so-called Millennial way? For starters, it's not a secret sauce or packet of magical beans. It's not a list of seven steps nor is it a well-trodden path. Surprisingly, it's a series of three significant shifts, or phases, that occur in one's life, if you allow them. These three shifts are: Step Up, Step Out, and Step Forward.

STEP UP

Step Up means taking inventory of the skills, tools, and infrastructure at your disposal and setting out on the journey. For Alex Rawitz, he Stepped Up by recognizing a need for the voiceless. For Anu Menon, she perceived the importance of her morning ritual. For Jordan DePaul, he moved to Nashville to submerge himself in the music scene.

At some point, these Millennials had a vague idea of what they wanted to do with their lives: entrepreneurship, business, music, etc. Then a transformation happened, and they stopped thinking and started doing.

Some folks call this transformation "taking the leap," but I think it's something much more than that. It's getting off your butt, Stepping Up, and taking action!

At first glance, this change in attitude may seem like the easiest step. However, countless Millennials are still hung up on their dream. They never Stepped Up and took action, and thus, they still feel incomplete, as if they aren't entirely the person they want to be. In this chapter, I'll provide you with the tools to stop dreaming and start doing.

STEP OUT

You can't have a clay pot without first firing it in a kiln. The same goes for our personal journeys. If you want to be successful, you need to put yourself out there. An artist can paint a picture, but it doesn't become a masterpiece until it's hung before the public's eye.

After Stepping Up, the Millennials I've been fortunate enough to interview Stepped Out into the world. Vulnerable and exposed, they bared their ideas, talents, and skills for the world to ridicule.

"I want to run a startup," said Alex Rawitz. "We want to create a high-end coffee company," said Anu Menon and Suyog Mody. Friends and family resisted. They tried to shield their loved ones from the criticism of the world, but because these Millennials were cast into the kiln, they became stronger.

This chapter will help you overcome the obstacles holding you back from Stepping Out into the world.

STEP FORWARD

The most important shift is Step Forward. As Bilbo says in *The Fellowship of the Ring*, "You step onto the road, and if you don't keep your feet, there's no knowing where you might be swept off to."

If you become stagnant, other forces will take the helm and steer you in the wrong direction. You must move forward. Once you are out, there is no turning back. Even if this road on which you've embarked leads to failure, you can still learn something and take a new road. Just like the layout of a great city, there are many roads one can choose at any given moment.

Lisa Kirk didn't give up when Southern Weddings Magazine denied her internship application. Alex didn't throw in the towel when every incubator turned his company down. Instead, Lisa sought out more internships and Alex applied to more programs. Eventually, they both arrived where they intended. Maybe their route involved detours, but they continued to Step Forward.

Although your journey may never come to a complete end, this book will have to at some point. Therefore, in the parting chapter, I leave you with advice to help keep you going.

THE SYSTEM IS BROKEN

I originally intended this book to be a pat on the back for Millennials, something older generations could use to face their preconceived notions about us, but I realized that would be selfish. The more I talked with folks from older generations, the more I noticed a recurring theme: no matter our age, we all feel stuck at some point in our life. Maybe you need to work to pay off debts and put food on the table. Maybe you've never had anyone believe in you or show you encouragement. Maybe you've given up thinking you were meant to chase your dream.

Whatever the situation, there is always a way forward. I know at first this may seem like an over-simplification of what it takes to achieve your dream, but many of us are still stuck waiting to Step Up. I've met too many people in my career who are unhappy with their jobs but are unwilling to do anything about it. I'm here to help you get un-stuck.

Today, nearly 71% of the American workforce is disengaged from their jobs. That means three out of four people wake up unhappy to go to work. So who makes up the 1 in 4 people who are happy and engaged at work? I'm going to venture a guess that these folks are not afraid to take risks, are ambitious to follow their dreams, and are willing to disprove the naysayers.

In my research for this book, I've encountered many Millennials who fit this mold. The Millennial generation is poised to reinvent the workforce with our technological acumen, willingness to try new things, and ability to create. This new Millennial way will one day replace the archaic notions we've subscribed to for the past century and launch us into a prosperous future.

If you are ready to learn the Millennial way and change your life for the better, read on.

CHAPTER 1: STEP UP

I have a theory that as we get older, we value our dreams less and less. But as we get older, we theoretically should have more resources at our disposal to achieve our dreams than when we were younger. Of course, there are a few exceptions to this theory. You know what I am talking about. You log into Facebook and see another friend who quit her full-time job to travel. Or your cousin who you thought was just an "aspiring filmmaker" shares his Kickstarter campaign to help fund a legit film. Somewhere in the constant stream of self-promotion and cat videos, ordinary people you know are sharing a serious message that we're not waiting anymore. We're ready to chase our dreams.

"I wish that could be me," you mutter to yourself while scrolling through your feed, hoping something else will come along to distract you.

So what sets these dream-chasers apart? Do you ever wonder why some people can just Step Up and chase their dream? Did they receive a big break or stroke of good luck? Nope, they did something simple. At some point, these people had a vague idea of what they wanted to do with their lives – writing, music, business, etc. Then they stopped thinking and started doing.

Stepping Up means taking inventory of the skills, tools, and infrastructure at your disposal and setting out on the journey. It means refining our current skills and learning new ones. It means curating resources and seeking out mentors. It means saying "I am a..." instead of "One day I hope to be a..."

My son recently learned how to stand up. Nothing fancy. He simply crawls up to a stationary (and hopefully secured) object and begins to pull himself up. It's obvious the next stage of his development will be walking, but it would be ridiculous for me to assume my son could walk right away after just learning to stand. The same applies to us. Yes, the initial Stepping Up process may feel clumsy. We will fall on our butts over and over, but, like my son, we will keep trying. It may be tempting to compare yourself to those who are already walking toward their dream, but learning to Step Up is critical for our journey.

Retrospectively, taking the first step toward your dream is always the easiest. But when you are on the other side, looking forward toward what you want to accomplish, you might as well be wearing concrete boots. The first step seems insurmountable. However, the first step is more manageable than you think. It involves a change in mindset as well as a concrete plan. In some cases, it's as simple as gathering information or meeting with a mentor.

In this chapter you will learn to give yourself permission to dream, overcome the fear holding you back, and put together a practical plan utilizing the "80/20 Rule" to Step Up and chase your dream. Are you ready to Step Up? I already know you are. Why else would you be reading this book?

1.1 PERMISSION TO DREAM

I was told from an early age the key to a happy life is a steady paycheck, a mortgage, and a white picket fence. At the same time, I was told I could become anything I wanted to be.

Whether to protect my innocence or project their failed ambitions on me, the mentors of my youth failed to inform me that few people make a living doing what they love. For most Millennials, we arrived at an entirely different landscape than what our mentors foreshadowed. Instead of following our dreams, we were thrust head first into the rat race to pay off our student loans, make rent, and still find a way to feed ourselves. Before long, life suffocated our dreams. Slowly, our dreams faded into the abyss, waiting for us to chase them later when life is less complicated.

I've already lived through one failed dream. Six summers ago, after I finished my sophomore year at Pitt, I split my time as a courier for a local medical office and as an intern at a film and television studio. The courier job didn't pay well, but it was enough to support a dream I had since high school: make it in the *film biz.*

The plan worked flawlessly. With few responsibilities and only a couple bills to pay, I was free to focus on my dream. As the summer came to a close, I knew the following year would be my big break. But the pursuit didn't last long. As my junior year drew on, life nudged its way between me and my dream. I took a *real* internship at a *real* company. It was the responsible thing to do; I needed to start thinking about my future. So I spent the following summer taking classes and working, thinking all the while that the next summer would be my big break. It never came.

Instead of taking my dream out back and putting it out of its misery, life cruelly let it die a slow and painful death. I don't dream of working in the film biz anymore, but its ghost still haunts me. Life is unfair like that. For some of us, our dreams held on for dear life. You might not realize this, but subconsciously you've already Stepped Up to chase your dream. How many times have you said to yourself, "One day I will..." or, "Someday I'd like to be a..."? Deep down, this is your soul speaking to you, crying out to fulfill what she is meant to do. Hidden away in the background, underneath the facade you've built to shield you from the truth is the ugly admission that you're not happy with your life's trajectory. It's okay. Use this as your launching point. It's time for you to take the first step.

It's time for you to start dreaming again.

STOP DRIFTING THROUGH LIFE

Growing up, I was a smart kid. I graduated in the top 10% of my class, I earned the rank of Eagle Scout, and I excelled in math and science. So naturally I studied engineering in college and landed the first two jobs I ever interviewed for – all before my 25th birthday. And here I am, halfway through my twenties, realizing this isn't what I wanted all along – all because it was the practical path. My mistake? I failed to give myself permission. Permission to dream.

Why does one have to give themselves permission to dream? If we don't dream, we don't set goals. If we don't set goals, we don't put plans in place. If we don't put plans in place, we will drift through life from one mediocre task to the next. Meandering through life is not the way I want to live, nor was it for Anu Menon and Suyog Mody, the duo behind the up-and-coming coffee subscription company Driftaway Coffee.

After years of working at good tech jobs, Anu and Suyog grew tired of living comfortable but predictable lives.

"We just had this itch to do something. After a couple years of working, it was time for a change," Anu told me. Sensing there was something missing, they embarked on a journey to find their purpose.

Anu and Suyog met in college in 2002 and worked for the same company after graduation. Following stints in Atlanta, London, and finally New York, Anu decided to take a six-month sabbatical away from the corporate world.

"When we came back to New York, I was trying to figure out what I wanted to do. I was dabbling in a few different things. I knew I wanted something different, so the first thing is to just try something out and figure out what I was good at and enjoyed doing," Anu said. Her sabbatical gave her the freedom to reflect on her life and examine what truly made her happy.

Looking back at your passion projects, the dynamic relationships you've developed, or the books you've recommend to friends, you begin to gather a clearer picture of the direction in which you want your life to travel.

For Anu, she didn't have to look too far past her morning routine. "Our morning coffee became less about just caffeine and convenience, and more about a ritual we relished," their website reads. Driftaway Coffee was born.

Dream the Life You Want

When did you stop dreaming? I'm serious, when? Not so long ago when "adults" asked us what we wanted to be when we grow up, we could get away with saying something silly like a ballerina-astronaut, Batman, or ghost hunter. How old were you when you stopped giving these answers and started repeating what you thought other people would find interesting?

For me, it was around middle school when I decided to "grow up" and learn to live in the "real world." While scheduling classes for my freshman year of high school, I dropped all my art classes to take mechanical- and engineering-based classes. This was the practical approach. The responsible decision adults make. Unfortunately, I can't go back in time to tell younger Declan not to be afraid of chasing his dream. And to be honest, I wouldn't want to. I don't believe in living with regrets; the only thing I can change is me in the present moment. The same applies to all of us. If you are tired of the cubicle lifestyle, stop regretting your decision to go to school for accounting. If you wished you had more time to travel the world, stop fretting about the student loans you have to pay off. Right now, right this moment, you can Step Up, and give yourself permission to dream.

Now, please note that I'm not bashing non-creative professions such as lawyers, doctors, or engineers. The world still needs these professions, and there are some people whose dream it is to become one of these professions. Honestly, I actually enjoy engineering and the chance to tickle the analytical side of my brain. Except this isn't what I *want* to do; it doesn't fulfill my purpose in life. I only discovered this about two years ago after I began to dream again. I didn't know it at the time, but I wanted to be a writer. After years of regretting the path I chose, I let go of my regret and gave myself permission to dream. Here I am a few years later with my first book. I couldn't have done it if I stopped thinking practically and started dreaming instead.

In the next section, I will talk about the fears that hold us back from dreaming and even cripple us from taking action to chase our dream. But before moving on, please take some time to reflect on the following questions.

REFLECTION QUESTIONS:

1. What did you want to be when you were young?

2. If money, time, or resources were not an issue, what would you do right this moment?

3. Why did you stop dreaming?

1.2 OVERCOMING FEAR

Alex had a great idea.

Alex Rawitz and his friend identified a common problem with modern news media: the lack of Millennial perspective conveyed in a compelling and engaging manner. From the Occupy Movement to the Ferguson Riots, Alex wanted to hear the stories from the ignored sources, those often drowned out by the "noise." Not only did he identify this shortfall, but he found himself in the heart of Silicon Valley with the resources and knowledge base to turn this shortfall into a solution. Possibly even turn it into a real product.

However, with a year remaining at Stanford to finish his English degree and a lifetime of parents' expectations of graduating from a prestigious school weighing him down, Alex contemplated letting someone else solve the media problem. How could he run a startup? How would he tell his parents? What if he failed? Every bad scenario played on loop inside Alex's head.

Even if we manage to give ourselves permission to dream, there still exists something holding us back, preventing us from moving forward. Author Steven Pressfield coined the term "Resistance," but I like to call it what it really is: fear. Fear cripples action. For a lot of us, the initial rush of joy from the idea of our dream is wiped out by the crushing fear that follows. Fear makes us play it safe. Instead of Stepping Up, we hide behind phrases like, "I hope to do that...someday," or, "If I didn't work full-time I'd be a..."

Not for Alex. Alex is an exception. He couldn't shake the "rush," and more importantly, couldn't give up on his purpose: giving voice to the voiceless. So with all the unknown possibilities and possible failures ahead, Alex overcame his fears and Stepped Up to chase his dream.

Taking a year off from school, Alex and the Verbatm team were accepted into a San Francisco-based incubator and are now about to release a fully functional prototype "to a final round of collegiate beta testers across the country." Alex and his team went back to school to finish their degrees. However, they are all committed to the entrepreneur's path.

I asked Alex what's next, and he replied, "We're in talks with an investor who might potentially bankroll a significant chunk of the 500K we're looking to raise in order to hire engineers and partner with media organizations/content creators. So all in all, exciting times!"

Although one could argue Alex's young age played a role in his naive ignorance, he bravely mastered his fear of the unknown, rejection, and failure.

FEAR OF THE UNKNOWN

For our ancient ancestors, the unknown was something they feared. So they invented fire, to give them a bit more visibility in the darkness.

It's different nowadays, though. When we live a comfortable life with a steady paycheck, a good partner, and maybe even a cat or two, it can be hard to imagine a life with the uncertainty that accompanies chasing your dream. It's difficult for me. I live a complacent life; my job is comfortable, my lifestyle is simple, and my car is a Rogue. Life is good. Why would I want to mess that up?

What would happen, let's say, if I achieved my dream of becoming a writer and being self-employed? Well, I'm sure my lifestyle would change. I might have to work more to support my family. I might have to travel and be away from my wife and son more often. I might worry a lot more. Sometimes success is just as scary as failure. I don't know what will happen if I chase my dream, and this unknown variable frightens me.

Basically, fear of the unknown equates to the fear of living. Life is one big unknown and every day we venture out, waiting to see what surprises may come our way. People who are afraid of the unknown are people who are afraid to live.

Imagine the regret of never chasing your dream. Weigh that thought against your fear. Like I mentioned earlier in this chapter, I don't want to live a life full of regrets. I'd rather regret less and fear more than regret more and fear less. For Alex, he needed to get his startup idea out of him. He couldn't imagine living life knowing he didn't give it a shot. So he went for it, head-on into the deep uncertainty.

FEAR OF REJECTION

Someone important once said a prophet is not welcome in his hometown. The same rings true in today's modern world. Those closest to us often are the first to question our dreams. Their questioning often shapes our self-identity. The expectations others have for us affect our own personal expectations. Thus, as we dream of a different "me," we fear rejection from those closest to us.

On the other hand, we possess something inside all of us that we want to share and have the world appreciate. Maybe you fancy backpacking across the Alps instead of going to law school. Maybe you want to be a filmmaker instead of an accountant. But instead of chasing your dream, you play it safe in fear of being "misunderstood."

It's a catch-22: the world knows us by what we do with our life, but our life has been predetermined by the world. Let me stop right now and say that if people are holding you back from chasing your dream, confront them. You should never tolerate others' resistance from allowing you to achieve your dreams.

Although the struggle is real, it mainly exists in our heads. If you are surrounded by loving and supportive friends and family, no matter their expectations, I guarantee you have nothing to fear. Share your dream. Overcome your fear of rejection.

FEAR OF FAILURE

Failure is my favorite fear. Why? Because I've learned to harness this fear into fuel to power my metaphorical dream chasing engine.

Before chasing your dream, you need to accept one simple fact: you will fail along the way. All of the greats, from Albert Einstein to Jonas Salk, from Michael Jordan to Matt Damon, have failed at one point, but that never held them back. Failure only made them better.

You can measure success by your ability to accept failure; if you can do this, you will clear the biggest hurdle in your way.

Failure can be detrimental, I understand. However, there are ways to mitigate failure. I have faith that with a cool demeanor, critical thinking skill set, and ability to learn and adapt, there is nothing anyone should fear.

In my line of work we have something called the Failure Mode Analysis. In essence, it's a way to evaluate all the possible outcomes of a product or service and put in place contingency plans to limit the damage.

The same philosophy can be applied to your life. Are you afraid of losing your job? Save up money and keep in touch with contacts at other companies. Worried about your health? Start an exercise habit and eat healthier. Anxious about chasing your dream? Find a mentor to help guide you through the initial steps. The ability to predict failure leads to a life lived without fear.

Make a plan, execute said plan to the best of your ability, make necessary adjustments, complete and move on.

Life is too short to live in fear. Failure is progress. Failure is potential.

HAPPY-YOU

The struggles Alex faced were a mixture of the three types above. However, his biggest hurdle was living a life not in conformity with his parents' expectations. When I asked Alex how his parents felt that he took a year off to chase his dream, he said:

"My dad actually told me he'd almost rather me put out a book or something I could have my name to than just a business that made a lot of money. Which I thought was interesting because they had never vocalized that or encouraged me, they didn't want to put those expectations on me or have me live with that burden. I realized that was still really present in their minds.

"At the end of the day, they're not displeased or unhappy. They've never forbidden me from doing any of this, with the promise to graduate, which I was totally on board with. I think it would be silly to not have the degree after putting in the work for it. But they see that I am happy and they see that I'm productive and working on something. They're happy, you know, it's an interesting chapter of my life and they are curious to see what happens to it."

Doing something you love brings out the real you, the real you people will want to see. Even if they are used to engineer-you, accountant-you, or lawyer-you, they will unquestionably welcome happy-you.

REFLECTION QUESTIONS:

1. What do you fear most about your journey?

2. How has fear hampered you in the past?

3. Are your fears based on past experiences or do they stem from what you think might happen?

1.3 Chasing Your Dream on the Side - The 80/20 Rule

"How can I pursue my dream if I still have a full-time job?"

It's an honest question; one I personally struggle with answering. The ugly truth is you have to find the margin in your life. And if you don't have the margin, make some.

To clarify, I'm not talking about the margins you adjust on your research paper to help you hit the 10-page minimum requirement. If you are unfamiliar with the term, margin refers to the time between scheduled events in your life. For example, the time after putting my son to bed and 10 PM is my "creative" margin. The late evening is the time I set aside to work on what I am passionate about – writing.

In a way, we all subconsciously plan what we do with the margins in our life. If we have a few minutes of free time, we fill it with checking our Facebook or Snapchat. If an hour or so frees up, we might veg out on the couch to catch an episode or two of *Seinfeld*. But are we using our margins efficiently? If you've given yourself permission to dream, if you've overcome your fear holding you back, I can promise you will find the time. But first, you have to take control of your life and utilize your margins.

Life is sneaky. It creeps up on you, slowly crowding out your dreams and ambitions. If you don't keep life in check, it may obliterate your dreams altogether. For example, take a typical day for me two years ago. It was probably another long day at work. As I came in through the door, I threw down my bag and plopped down on the couch, and then I remained there for the majority of the evening.

Oh crap, I haven't written a blog post yet, I thought. It was pointless. I had the time, but my mind was shot. So I put Netflix on to help fill the void. Erica joined me and we wasted away the night. I woke up the next day and repeated the same process.

This was March of 2014, a time filled with stress from work and a complete lack of creative juice to keep our Cooking in College blog functional. Now you might read this and think it sounds quite ordinary, which it is. We all have these days. However, "one of those days" turned into "every single day" for me! I was stuck in a horrible routine, and I know some of you reading this are in the same situation.

The struggle we face is not having enough time to chase our dream. No, the struggle is failing to define what to do with our time so we can use it intentionally. First, we need to set boundaries. Once the boundaries are set, we can find the ways for our dreams and life responsibilities to coexist. One of the greatest struggles I see young people facing is whether to follow a less lucrative dream or take a well-paying job. What young people fail to realize is the third option.

Do both.

You Say Potato, I Say Pareto

There doesn't have to be a choice between a secure job and chasing your dream. You can do both. But I'm going to be frank: chasing your dream on the side takes a lot of work and dedication. A lot.

However, I've worked out a way to practically pursue a dream and make a living. It's a system that has worked well for me over the past few years. In my native field of study in industrial engineering, we have a concept called the Pareto Principle, also known as the 80/20 Rule. In layman terms, the 80/20 Rule means 80% of your profits come from 20% of your products.

It also applies to a wide variety of situations, but for our sake, I've found the 80/20 rule strikes the right balance between living life and pursuing a dream. I'm awake for 16 hours in any given day (sometimes more when my son is teething), and 80% of my time is spent making a living and taking care of life's responsibilities while the other 20% is spent pursuing my dream. If you don't want to do the math: 13 hours on life and 3 hours on my dreams.

It may seem small, but if you are dedicated and intentional with your time, you'll be surprised how much you can accomplish. Extrapolate my figures across a whole year and you get 1,095 hours to chase your dream. That's the equivalent of working full-time for 27 weeks dedicated to nothing but chasing your dream. Think about it, by committing 20% of your waking time working on your dream you essentially have half a year's worth of full-time-dream-chasing at your disposal.

Personally, I'm able to spend a solid hour writing a day, with the rest of my three hours split up in smaller increments learning, networking, reading, or brainstorming. Last year I was able to increase my number of subscribers eleven-fold and grow my Twitter following by 600%. I systematically used the time available to build my business. Progress is possible.

FROM 80/20 TO STEPPING OUT

Remember Anu and Suyog of Driftaway Coffee from the first section of this chapter? Well, they didn't recklessly follow their dream; they were practical with their approach.

"If you are dreaming of something, start it on the side," Anu said. "We started working on Driftaway in July of 2013. At that point I was working on it full-time and Suyog was still working full-time at the consulting company. He would work [on Driftaway] in the evenings, occasionally, and on the weekends."

While Anu slowly pieced together Driftaway Coffee, Suyog strategically created margin in his schedule to help out as much as he could.

"I had to limit and start putting in fixed times to leave the office. Realistically, on the weekdays, we ended up working maybe two to three hours together. We would do something during the day, like create a logo for instance, and then (in the evening) we'd look at it together for a half-hour and keep working on it."

Slow and steady, Anu and Suyog pieced together the framework of Driftaway Coffee. They still had life responsibilities, but they dedicated their margins to chasing their dream. It's amazing how much they accomplished with a bit of focused dedication. For example, in one weekend, Anu and Suyog retrofitted a popcorn machine they bought on Amazon to roast coffee beans. A small but necessary step for a budding coffee company.

"It was a lot of small, small steps," Suyog told me. However, the constant back and forth of focusing on his consulting work and Driftaway wore him down.

"One day I am thinking of consulting projects, the other day I'm thinking about Driftaway Coffee. [My focus] just kept switching. I was like, 'This is all very conflicting because I don't want to do a sucky job in one place and then try to give a lot of attention to the other.'"

As the end of Anu's sabbatical loomed over them, Suyog knew he needed to leave his job to take Driftaway to the next level. So in August of 2014, without a grand exit, Suyog quietly left his consulting job to focus solely on Driftaway. "It was nice to finally pay attention to one thing."

I don't want to de-emphasize Anu and Suyog's accomplishment, but it's incredible what you can achieve with a few dedicated hours a week, a couple sacrificed weekends, and one popcorn machine. Suyog left me with some parting advice:

"Your work is going to fill a large part of your life, and the only way to be truly satisfied is to do what you believe is great work. And the only way to do great work is to love what you do. If you haven't found it yet, keep looking."

If you've found it, it's time to stop looking, and time to Step Out.

REFLECTION QUESTIONS:

1. How much margin do you have in your weekly schedule?

2. Do you find the balance between productivity and leisure in your margins?

3. What are you willing to sacrifice to start taking your dreams seriously?

CHAPTER 2: STEP OUT

If you want to be successful in life, you need to put yourself out there. Like I said in the introduction, a clay pot must first be cast into a hot kiln if it is to become useful to anyone. For our purposes, this means we must cast ourselves into the world by sharing our dreams, becoming vulnerable and stronger all the while. By putting yourself in the world's view, you prove to yourself and to others you are ready for success and possess the necessary skills to accomplish what you set out to do.

Once you have made the conscious effort to Step Up by giving yourself permission to dream, overcoming fear, and making a solid plan to chase your dream on the side, you are then ready to move into the next phase: Step Out.

Stepping Out onto your journey is rapid, unforgiving, and full of failure. The more pain you experience, the more times you fail, the closer you are to achieving your dream. You can accept failure. Failure is progress. Are you ready for the cuts and scrapes that accompany failure? Are you ready to say, with confidence, "This is what I'm doing with my life"? If not, revisit Step Up; most likely fear is still holding you back. But to achieve your dream, you have to pass through the refining fire eventually.

When you officially Step Out into the real world, you are no longer safe. You are now a target. People will continue to doubt you. They will try to bring you down because of their past failures. These people don't know how to fail. You do. Not only are you a target for criticism, but opportunities will fly right into your face. If you aren't prepared to catch one, it will fly past you. However, the gut instinct to go after the right opportunities will develop as you encounter more and more decisions. Luck comes into play, but you are still in control of preparing for opportunities.

In this chapter, you will meet Lisa Kirk and hear the story of how she landed her dream job of writing for a prominent wedding magazine simply by starting a blog. Advised by a college professor not to chase the unlikely possibility of landing a job in magazine publishing, Lisa ferociously went after her dream instead. You will also meet singer-songwriter Jordan DePaul, who overcame friction as he journeyed toward his dream of becoming a recording artist in Nashville. Instead of accepting a job promotion at an established performing rights organization, Jordan quit his job to focus full-time on his music. I will then close on how harnessing vulnerability helps you overcome the expectations of others.

Are you ready to Step Out? I'm not speaking metaphorically; I'm talking about putting practical plans in place to Step Out into the world with your dream. The world is waiting.

2.1 SHOWCASE YOUR DREAM

"I was the girl who made writing clubs with her friends."

That's Lisa Kirk, currently one of the editors of *Southern Weddings Magazine*. At the start of this book project, I eyed one Millennial in particular who epitomized the Step Up, Step Out, and Step Forward journey: Lisa. I've followed Lisa's journey vicariously through my wife Erica since the time they met in college. Lisa is a unique Millennial. She is willing to be patient and work hard to achieve her goals rather than expecting instant results.

Lisa grew up in a home that valued books, Lisa always knew she wanted to be a writer, but after discovering *American Girl*'s January/February 2000 issue, she knew she wanted to write for a magazine.

"I went to college thinking I wanted to work for a lifestyle publication like *Southern Living*." So when an internship opened up at *Southern Living*, Lisa applied. However, *Southern Living* turned her down, informing Lisa to gain more experience first.

So, without many opportunities in Steubenville, Ohio, Lisa transferred to the nearby University of Pittsburgh and landed an internship with *Pittsburgh Magazine*. "*Pittsburgh Magazine* was my first big magazine experience. It was so rewarding. They were working on their annual weddings edition at the time, and I was really interested in fashion and interior design." Lisa, a self-proclaimed "hopeless romantic," discovered a whole new field of magazine writing: weddings.

It was through this internship that Lisa also found blogging. Soon after the semester ended, Lisa started her own wedding blog, Something Pretty. For three years, she blogged five times a week about weddings with the intent of landing a job at a major wedding publication. Lisa took advantage of the pre-Pinterest and pre-Instagram era to develop her signature style, study the industry, and understand the major players.

Lisa held her sights on one major player in particular, *Southern Weddings*. "I had been reading [*Southern Weddings*] ever since I discovered wedding blogs. They put so much emphasis on the marriage and not just the wedding. I loved what *Southern Weddings* was doing."

Through her blog, Lisa interacted with *Southern Weddings* by commenting on their blog posts, tweeting to them, and entering their contests. "Emily Thomas (Creative Director) began to comment occasionally on Something Pretty, so I knew she knew I existed."

Not only did Lisa garner the attention of thousands through her blog, she also earned the attention of an influential few. Without bravely Stepping Out, Lisa wouldn't have been able to approach Emily in a more formal way a few months before graduation.

"I told her a little bit about what my experience was, what my goals were, and that I hopefully wanted to work for *Southern Weddings*, and so I asked her what I could be doing in my last semester in college that will make me the best candidate I could be if something were to come up."

This proactive approach paid off for Lisa. About a month later, Emily reached out to Lisa for a possible opening and asked if she was interested. Since the *Southern Weddings* team is made up of only a few women, they comb through candidates to make sure everyone can "vibe" with each other. For Lisa, this meant sitting through five interviews over the course of three months.

Graduation came and went for Lisa, and she still had not heard back from her dream job. "I was checking my email excessively." As the weeks dragged on, Lisa needed to distract herself and find creative ways not to keep checking her phone. Going to the movies with her mom and sister was a favorite tactic of hers. One day at the movies, as the credits for *The Great Gatsby* rolled, Lisa couldn't wait any longer and whipped out her phone. Sitting in her inbox was an unread email from *Southern Weddings*. She got the job.

"I burst into tears. It was such a joyful moment because everything I had been working toward paid off. I put all my eggs in one basket, which retrospectively I know isn't the best idea, but I felt confident that this is what the Lord was calling me to."

When I asked Lisa for the best advice to achieve your dreams, she said, "I was in the right place at the right time. You can't control that, but what you can control is having the right preparation. You never know when that right time and place is going to come, but you can control how prepared you are for when that happens."

Now it's your turn
Lisa did something many of us Millennials have failed to do: land a dream job that fills us with purpose and passion. Even with the small odds of landing an editorial role for a prominent magazine, Lisa still showed up five times a week for three straight years writing about weddings, gathering resources, and building a community around her.

By Stepping Out into the world, Lisa earned the trust of her readers who valued her input and perspectives. With this practice, Lisa was able to refine her writing skills and develop her signature style. Needless to say, without Something Pretty, no one at *Southern Weddings* would have known Lisa or even given her a chance.

After hearing Lisa's story, I hope you are determined to prepare yourself for opportunities that may arise. Stop expecting instant results and be willing to embrace the fact that no matter how hard you work toward your dream, luck still has a role to play. Your time will come, too, but in the meantime, do everything you can to prepare for when it does. Preparation naturally arises from Stepping Out and showcasing your work for the world to critique and provide feedback.

Lisa's journey is not over. She still has a life ahead of her full of new hopes and dreams. She will encounter many more twists and turns. As we travel toward the horizon of success, without managing friction, we will fail to enjoy the journey along the way. In the next section, we will review the types of friction that slow us down and the ways we can manage it.

REFLECTION QUESTIONS:
1. What is one way you can Step Out and "showcase" your dream to the world?

2. If you could do one thing five times a week for three years to achieve your dream, what would that one thing be?

3. If you could ask Lisa one thing about her journey, what would you ask?

2.2 MANAGING FRICTION

Having a dream is easy.

The hard part is putting actions into motion that will help turn your dream into reality. Once things are in motion, once you have Stepped Out and are actively chasing your dream, something begins to hold you back or slow you down. This invisible force is called friction. Friction prevents us from building the momentum we need to complete our projects, live out our dreams, and create the lives we want. Therefore, if we want to accomplish our goals, we need more than motivation. We need to reduce friction.

I'm not an avid bowler, but two or so times a year my wife and I will meet up with friends at one of the hipster bowling alleys in Pittsburgh (you know, the one with the classy cocktail bar and mixologist in suspenders). The concept of bowling is simple: hurl an object toward a set of other objects and knock them down. By exerting a force on a heavy ball, you create momentum. The ball then exerts another force on the pins, knocking them down. Awkward fist pumps and high fives ensue. It's simple physics. Or is it?

There is a growing sentiment among thought-leaders that motivation is the driving force behind everything we do. I get it, motivation is necessary to put things in motion. But people are quick to dismiss the other natural phenomena that occur in physics when applying a force to an object: friction. Friction acts against the exerted force. The same happens in life. Conventional thinking says, "If we are motivated enough, we will reach our goal." However, as we apply motivation to our project, we experience resistance that slows us down, sometimes dragging us to a complete stop before attaining our goal.

There is a reason we hurl round balls and not cubes and why maintenance folks slick the lanes with oil. These tactics are used to reduce friction so the ball can strike the pins with more force. The inventors of this fun pastime recognized the need to manage friction to accomplish their goal.

I'll hop off the physics analogy train for now and talk in more concrete terms. Over this past year, I created an eCourse, wrote this eBook, and launched a podcast. During each venture, I found three areas exerting friction on the desire to finish my project: fear, work ethic, and mood. These three things slowed my progress, drained my momentum, and caused unwarranted amounts of stress. But as the year went on, I learned to manage these three resistances. I stopped thinking about how others perceived me and put out content my readers needed to read. I set in place a writing schedule to overcome my "lack of time." And I practiced a pre-writing routine to make sure I was in the right mood to create. I didn't succumb to the friction; I didn't allow it to slow me down. I managed it.

An Artist's Struggle with Friction

Friction can come from several sources. It may be circumstantial and out of your control, it may arise from friends or family, or it may manifest internally.

Out of all those who dream, artists face the toughest forms of friction. Not only is funding for arts programs in public schools decreasing, but by the nature of their work, many artists come face to face with their inner demons. Doubt, negative self-worth, and fear drain the creative juices needed to produce good art. The lack of a stable income plays a role, too. A delicate, but necessary, balance exists between making a living and creating art. Tread too far in one direction and you'll sell out; in the other, you'll starve. That's why today many artists pursue their dream on the side, usually taking a nine-to-five and spending what little margin they have on their passion.

All this rang true for singer/songwriter Jordan DePaul of Nashville. While making a quick stop in Pittsburgh to play at a local wine bar, Jordan visited my home with his touring partner, Brittany Kennell (yes, the same Brittany Kennell from Season 10 of NBC's *The Voice*). I know Jordan through a mutual friend and consider him a good friend and inspiration.

Jordan studied marketing at Youngstown State University in Ohio before graduating in 2012. In early 2013, he moved to Nashville with no money, no job, no connections, and nowhere to stay. He landed an internship at Broadcast Music Incorporated as a business development specialist – a job he dreamed of and applied to all throughout college. However, Jordan quickly realized his heart wasn't into the work, but in his music.

"I'd go to work every day and I'd be on the phone and computer, then [on the side] I'd be on my laptop doing [my] music."

After twelve months, the company offered Jordan another position, but he turned it down. Jordan knew he couldn't serve two masters. "As soon as I quit, the hustle became real." Jordan took corporate gigs where nobody listened, played shows at 2 AM even if it was just a couple songs, and hustled his way just to make rent. All of this didn't matter to Jordan because every day he got to wake up and do what he loves – create music.

As he finally gained momentum, Jordan encountered friction.

"It started to seem like I was gaining a lot of momentum after I quit my job because I was able to focus on my music and things started picking up," Jordan told me. "I went to this show, four months after I quit my job, and there were all these local acts doing exactly what I was doing. And I was thinking, 'Why aren't I on this? These guys are great, but I've never heard of them.'"

Envy crept into Jordan's mindset, a common problem for anyone chasing their dream; you are excited about the people who are doing similar things you are doing, but you also grow envious of their success.

"It happens to me all the time, I see my friends are doing killer stuff, and I'm really happy for them too, but at the same time, they're doing the same thing I'm doing. It's the luck of the draw almost. For a while I let that affect me, I kept thinking, 'I'm working so hard but for what? What are the chances people are going to know who I am?'"

Envy is a distraction. Envy is friction. However, this friction helped Jordan to realize his true purpose in pursuing a career in music.

"For that one person in the crowd who's like, 'Yeah, I know exactly what he's talking about.' If I continued to connect with people on that level, that's what helped me overcome [my envy]."

DON'T ELIMINATE FRICTION; MANAGE IT

Think of one goal you want to accomplish. Maybe it's losing weight or landing your dream job. Before you apply motivation to get the ball rolling (pun intended), identify the potential areas where you may feel friction. Write a list and set out to manage the friction before applying any motivation. Ask yourself what you can do to minimize the impact and then do it! For example, the lack of a particular skill set may be a form of friction preventing you from landing a dream job. However, now that you identified the friction, you can address it.

Be aware that not all friction is bad. If it didn't exist, we wouldn't be able to walk, drive or make fire! Friends and family tend to exert the highest amount of friction, but typically the right kind. In bowling, the lanes are slicked with oil except for the last few feet so the ball can grip into the wood and cut toward the center pin. Without friction, the ball would slip into the gutters. Your friends and family act as the necessary friction to keep you from straying too far out of the lane. Keep this in mind. The key is to identify friction that can serve as a guide rail and friction that sabotages your goals completely. Manage, but do not eliminate, the guide rail friction in your life. If you do so, you'll accomplish more with less resistance.

You've learned how to prepare yourself for the opportunities to come, how to manage friction due to your newfound momentum, but now it's time to learn the hardest part of Stepping Out: dealing with vulnerability.

REFLECTION QUESTIONS:

1. What types of friction have you experienced in the past?

2. Do your friends and family tend to exert friction or add momentum to your journey?

3. What methods of managing friction work best for you?

2.3 Expectations and Vulnerability

In January of 2015, NPR launched a fantastic new podcast called Invisibilia. In one of their early episodes, they focus on the expectations our culture has for blind people. To summarize, without spoiling the episode, our society expects blind people to be handicapped in most facets of their life. For example, would you expect a blind person to ride a bike? Probably not. But in fact they can, and several have debunked this myth by riding a bike using echolocation. These expectations have a profound impact on how blind people behave. In a way, our expectations define who these blind people become.

Expectations fulfill reality in all walks of life. My parents, family, teachers, and friends all shaped who I would later become. As I've said previously in this book, I grew up as an A+ student. I excelled at Calculus and Physics in high school and earned the rank of Eagle Scout. As a 17-year-old kid, I yielded to the pressures of my parents and teachers' expectations to become an engineer. In their mind, I fit the mold. Unfortunately, this was not the mold in which I wanted to take shape.

I'm going to venture a guess the same has happened to you in some way. Our generation doesn't realize it, but others' expectations of us shape our future. We possess an innate fear of not achieving what others expect us to do, and this fear interferes with significant decisions we face: what school should I go to, what job should I apply to, who should I marry? Many of us follow the invisible compass of others' expectations and find ourselves lost instead of where we want to be. Part of Stepping Out to chase our dream is to slow down and ask ourselves, "Is this where *I* want to be or where *they* want me to be?"

I've been asking myself this question a lot this year. As I reflect upon it, I realize I possess a creative bug behind my analytical engineering mind. Overshadowed by the practical analytical side of my brain, my creative side never made itself present until the end of my junior year of high school. Upon seeing a program about filmmaking, I bought a small camcorder and spent my entire summer shooting, editing, and writing silly little short films. During my college years, while studying industrial engineering, my creative outlet evolved from filmmaking to writing (writing is a less expensive hobby than film, especially for a college student). Filmmaking and writing were the creative outlets with which I wasn't expected to fall in love. Engineers don't love making stories; they love making bridges.

Don't let the fear of not living up to others' expectations shape you. I have lived 26 years in the shadow of this fear, but now I am forging my own path. In a way, I am following Norton Juster's advice from *The Phantom Tollbooth* (my wife's favorite book): "Expectations is the place you must always go to before you get to where you're going."

After talking with my Millennial counterparts, I've noticed a small trend begin to evolve. Many of us are bucking expectations to pursue a life we want and not a life expected of us. Anu and Suyog, from the first chapter, worked in the tech industry for years before they decided to quit and follow their passion of starting Driftaway Coffee. Alex Rawitz faced tough pressure from his family to stay in school and finish his English degree, but instead took a year off to pursue a startup with a few colleagues.

Challenging everyone's expectations of who you are supposed to be takes vulnerability and a touch of humility. There are, however, a few practical approaches you can take.

DON'T SAY ANYTHING, JUST DO IT.

You are under no obligation to reveal your plans to anyone. Actually, recent studies indicate keeping your goals to yourself might increase your chances of achieving them. However, scientific studies aside, you might simply be afraid of the backlash and think it will jeopardize your progress from fulfilling your dream. If that's the case, just start chasing and wait for questions later. My wife took this approach with her classmates in pharmacy school. We both wanted to start a family, but in an extremely competitive school, Erica's classmates would certainly second guess her decision. So we just did it regardless (no pun intended) and made a baby while she was still in school. We didn't have to explain our motives to anyone.

REEL THEM IN SLOWLY

Instead of opening up your entire master plan, try bringing those around you in slowly. "I started a small blog," or, "I'm working on a short essay," are simple examples to reveal slowly that your dream is to become a writer. "I'm taking an online course to learn more about sailing" is another way to warm your loved ones up to the idea that you have other interests besides your nine-to-five job. Blatantly saying, "I'm taking a year-long trip to backpack across Africa," might easily be toned down to, "I've been watching some documentaries about Nigeria on Netflix and hope to one day visit." By revealing the small bend in your path instead of the summit ahead of you, your loved ones will be able to accompany you more readily on your journey.

JUST TELL 'EM

Honesty is my favorite solution. Instead of dancing around superficial small talk when visiting friends and family, have some courage to tell the truth about your dream. Don't be afraid of opening up to others. Who knows, you might find that other people face the same desires to chase their dream. If you encounter second-guessing or unwanted "advice," realize these people love you and want what's best for you. They are afraid of seeing someone they care about fail. As long as you are honest, including the struggles you face regarding your dream, they will accept you know what's best for you.

TIME TO EMBRACE YOUR VULNERABILITY

The fresh sting of admitting your real dreams to loved ones still throbs. You're self-conscious. You feel awkward. You're exposed and vulnerable.

Congratulations, you've made it.

The feeling of vulnerability is the first sign you are on your way. It means you have moved past Stepping Out and are almost ready to Step Forward. But first, you need to learn to take courage and embrace your vulnerability. Temptations may arise on your journey to hide your struggles, to make it seem like everything is roses.

Don't.

Some people have different thoughts on this subject, but I'm a steadfast believer in acknowledging your shortcomings rather than building a facade. The fear of appearing stupid or ill-informed drives us to seek answers or solutions to problems on our own. But here is a fun fact: people like helping other people. Sure, it takes a slice of humble pie to admit you don't know the answer, but connecting with someone who might have the life experiences to help you is incredibly valuable. However, you need to embrace your vulnerability first before seeking the advice from someone ahead of you on their journey.

I've wasted too much time on my personal journey trying to figure things out on my own and pretending to be somebody I'm not. Once I learned to embrace vulnerability, my journey accelerated. In fact, I don't even notice my vulnerability anymore; it's part of me. If you are ready to swallow your pride and embrace who you truly are in this moment, then you are ready for the next stage.

We've finished with the first two steps toward chasing your dream. If you are already at this stage in your journey, that's normal, but don't linger too long. Stepping Out on the rooftops and shouting out your dream does not equate to chasing your dream. You have to move forward. Sadly, many give up during the next step of the journey because it is the longest and most grueling stage. Little do they know, they are so close to tasting the sweet satisfaction of becoming the person they want to be. If you are ready to taste the sweetness, it's time for you to Step Forward.

REFLECTION QUESTIONS:
1. What method of opening up to others about your dream do you prefer?

2. How have other's expectations of you slowed you down or hampered your journey?

3. How do you react when you feel vulnerable?

Chapter 3: Step Forward

Of all the stages, Step Forward is the longest, most grueling stage. Because of this, it may seem like little progress is being made. But there is hope. A steadfast patience is essential. Success isn't checkers; it's pieced together like a precarious game of Jenga.

To be honest, this is the stage where I currently find myself. I've been Stepping Forward for years now. It's monotonous and frustrating. At times, I've thought I "made it" only to realize I had arrived at a false summit and needed to continue Stepping Forward.

Don't give up now. Keep going.

At this stage, it becomes harder to gauge the slope rising toward the summit, but it's there, I promise you. You'll struggle to find the footholds, you'll be tempted to take shortcuts, but you'll find you are not alone. At this point on the path, other people journey alongside you. Many of them will become your new friends. A connection forged from your common struggles will form. You'll also serve as a beacon of inspiration for those just starting to Step Up. Don't be afraid of offering a guiding hand.

You are so close to becoming the person you were meant to become. Once you reach the summit, you will never be the same again.

In this chapter, you will learn to view success differently. Instead of seeing success as a point one must arrive at, success is more like a horizon, something you can see and reach. However, once you reach the horizon, there is yet another horizon to attain. In other words, success is arbitrary, so learning to love the journey is more relevant than reaching the destination.

I'll also cover the vicious imposter syndrome and how to overcome it. As you continue to find yourself in new environments, you will have the tendency to hold back, fearing that you are an imposter. You have every right to be here. Own it!

Finally, I wrap up this book with a message close to my heart: measure growth by gratitude. As you travel on your journey, at times it may feel you are making no progress. Instead of giving up hope, recognize how amazing it is that you were chosen to chase this dream. The more gracious you are, the better you will be at appreciating the successes when they come.

Every moment, every action we take has led us here. You are so close. You only need to keep Stepping Forward!

3.1 Success on the Horizon

How do you know when you've reached success?

If you haven't thought about this question before, it might be time to start taking it seriously. Look out to the metaphorical horizon for a moment. What do you see? When you reach the Step Forward phase, out in the distance, barely visible to the naked eye, is the thin horizon of success. Excited, you hurry along your journey toward it, but as you travel toward the horizon, you never quite reach it. You walk and walk and walk, maybe even reaching the original point you noticed a way back. However, when you look forward again, stretched out in front of you is yet another horizon. It never ends.

Success, like a horizon, is not a finish line. There will always be more horizon stretched out in front of you, out of reach. As we journey through life, we will end up at the point that was once the horizon. But up close, it will seem entirely different than what we expected. We will never be completely satisfied.

The real sin is keeping an eye on the horizon but failing to appreciate the path before us. If we tread upon the road of life in hopes of reaching the horizon but ignore the adventure along the way, we'll lose ourselves. This is the hardest part of Stepping Forward, the never-ending journey. For some, the thought of spending the rest of our life traveling toward the horizon is scary.

Millionaire William J. Feathersmith in the *Twilight Zone* episode, "Of Late I Think of Cliffordville," becomes so bored with his "success" that he makes a deal with the Devil to travel back in time to start life over again. As it turns out, Feathersmith failed to appreciate his life the first time around and makes a series of critical mistakes the second time, leading him back to the present as a poor, broke custodian. Take note of your journey, appreciate the hardships, and don't make a deal with the Devil.

Now that you have made it this far, temptations to take shortcuts or settle down and end your journey are abundant. You've entered dangerous territory. Constantly looking for the shortcuts leads to an unhealthy work ethic and mindset. I'm not so much concerned about the destination, but rather the man I want to be when I arrive. The experiences you collect along the journey are more valuable than the successes you attain.

When you finally reach your dream, I want you to appreciate what you worked so hard for. As long as there is a horizon, keep Stepping Forward!

Don't Compare Your Journey to Others'

As you keep Stepping Forward, there will come a time when you will look back and see how far you've come. You'll be proud and happy with your progress (as you should be). But the moment you start comparing yourself to others who are even farther along on their journey, you'll fall behind on yours. Don't compare your "behind-the-scenes" with everyone else's "highlight reel."

I for one am at fault for this.

The Millennials who felt they were called to do something with their lives and followed their calling inspire me. I love hearing encouraging stories about Millennials who chased their dreams (I based this book on only a fraction of these exceptional Millennials). They are hard to ignore and even harder not to put on a pedestal. We need to be careful not to hold these individuals in too high esteem. Like Jordan DePaul from chapter 2, I also experience the pangs of envy when I see other people succeeding around me. I know I am not alone.

What about those who haven't made it? What about those whose horizon is far off? What about the majority of our generation still stuck in a rut? What do we make out of our lack of our "success"?

Real success isn't about making lots of money or becoming famous. Real success, the kind you can be proud of, is about achieving what you were called to do. It's about following your true purpose.

CRACK OPEN THE BLACK BOX AND FIND YOUR PURPOSE

"Keep your head down and work hard," used to be the mantra echoed by generations past. If you were the first to show up and the last to leave, you were most likely the one tapped for the promotion. Older generations valued how much time you put into your work, how much you sacrificed, how loyal you were. On the flip-side, nowadays our generation prizes how much you've done with your life.

"Have you started a company? How many books have you written? What's your Twitter follower count?"

Produce more so we can consume more. Squeeze every ounce of free time into something productive. Input or output? Which generation had it right?

Neither.

In real life, I am a supply chain analyst. A supply chain is a series of inputs, processes, and outputs. To simplify things, we tend to call complex processes the black box. But in this game of life we play, what's in our black box?

Purpose. Purpose is at the center of input and output. Purpose drives our process. Without purpose, we're just a middleman in the cog of another person's agenda. The value people tie to themselves, by either how hard they work or how much they produce, bothers me. What people fail to realize is that in their black box, between inputs and outputs, lay something even more valuable – their true purpose. But how does one find their true purpose and crack open the black box? Ask yourself, "Why?"

Why did I write this book? Because I love sharing my thoughts and experiences with others.

Why? Because I hope it helps others find clarity in their struggles.

Why? Because helping people is good.

Why? Because people are good.

Why? Because...

"Why" is an annoying question; it gets under your skin. It scares you, but asking, "Why?" over and over again is the key to unlocking your black box. We each have our own answer. Be honest, does your answer scare you?

If your "why" doesn't scare you, you haven't thought hard enough. You should be so afraid of not achieving your "why" that every day of your life is zeroed in on achieving it. Your "why" is your purpose. It's the ultimate renewable energy. Ask yourself, "Why?" and then ask it again and again. Ask it five times over.

Find it. Embrace it. Live it.

Defining When We "Made it"

My dad grew up right outside Pittsburgh but moved to California when his father died. He worked as an electrician's apprentice and earned his union card in Los Angeles, and when he and my mother moved back to Pennsylvania to raise my sister and me, he was treated as an outsider by the local union. Work wasn't always abundant out here in Western Pennsylvania, and the union didn't make it easy for "travelers" to find employment. It was an unfortunate situation.

My mom worked part-time on and off when she could. She even earned a bachelor's degree during a challenging financial stretch and used her degree to land a part-time job, all while raising a family.

Over the years, my dad faced long stretches of unemployment, sometimes months at a time. The jobs he did work were often outdoors, at night, and exposed to the harsh Western PA winters. Being in grade school, I didn't completely understand the impact of losing a job, but I knew it wasn't good. Thanks to my mom's financial prowess and the sacrifices my parents made together, my sister and I never felt the impact of two unemployed parents. We grew up blissfully unaware.

My dad faced the elements to make ends meet. Through earth, wind and road salt, he struggled on. Even today, my dad still works a job he's unhappy at, but I guarantee if I ask him, "Was all this worth it?" he wouldn't hesitate to answer, "Yes."

My parents' story taught me that some of us just aren't called to make it, per se. I don't believe for one second my dad never amounted to anything or that he never succeeded. Why? Because the work was bigger than him, no matter how meaningless it appeared. Although the actual work he performed day to day might not have been important, his "why" mattered more - his family.

If you are like me and find yourself in a melancholy job, it's imperative (almost necessary) for us to realize the work is bigger than us. Maybe you also have a family to support. Or maybe you are pursuing a dream. All of us, for whatever reason, work for a bigger purpose. Failing to realize your "why" will only lead to unhappiness and despair throughout our careers. Your "why" may not be the same tomorrow or the next year (it's highly volatile to your circumstance), but over time, it will guide your definition of success.

It's time to redefine what it means to "make it." Sure, what I do every day has little importance to the world, but it has a significant importance for the family I support. That should mean something. My parents sacrificed so that my sister and I could grow up in a part of the world immune to outside pressure and away from the gang-ridden streets of LA; someplace where we could earn a good education and make something of ourselves. I'm happy to say because of their sacrifices, my life has been built on a solid foundation. My parents know this, and they are happy because they succeeded.

As hard as it is to support my wife, who is still in pharmacy school, and our son, I'm happy to accept this as part of my journey. I use every opportunity to grow and better myself. In the end, our journey, and not our dream, is what shapes us. In the hazy future before me, I can barely make out what I will amount to. However, I know there still lay a boundless horizon, but stretched out before that horizon is a long and arduous path, full of twists and turns, mountains and valleys, rivers and lakes.

I haven't "made it," but I'm sure as heck "making it."

REFLECTION QUESTIONS:

1. How did you originally view success?

2. What areas of your journey are hard to appreciate?

3. Do you have anyone in your life who is not the prototypical "success story" but is successful in your eyes?

3.2 Learning to Own it - Imposter Syndrome

One weekend last fall, while taking my son out for a walk, I passed six young children huddled around a gated fence.

The fence surrounded a well-manicured lawn, save for the neon orange soccer ball smack dab in the middle of it. Heads together, the children plotted what I assumed to be the rescue mission. One head popped up from the huddle upon my passing, but quickly it dived back to continue discussing the plan. From the huddle, the oldest child dragged the smallest to the gate and shoved him inside. He hesitated, but once a few moments passed, he stepped toward the ball. After three steps, fear overcame him and turning on his heel, the child bolted back to the gate.

I've been in this situation before. Many times in my youth I knocked a whiffle ball or two into my neighbor's garden. Retrospectively, I wasn't in any serious trouble, but this childhood fear of being someplace where I didn't belong still resonates with me today. Who am I to give advice on chasing your dreams or living a purposeful life? I haven't achieved my dream of self-employment, so why would anyone want to listen to me?

The fear those kids faced at the gated lawn is real. It affects us all even as we get older. We find ourselves in situations we imagine we aren't supposed to be. Maybe you manage a team of highly qualified co-workers. Maybe you joined a yoga class only to discover later on that "beginner class" meant having prior experience. Maybe you want to speak up about a social issue you care about but feel inadequate defending your position.

Instead of going after the ball, we flee back to the gate. We wait for permission to invite us in. Imposter syndrome is real, and if it affects us as kids, it definitely affects us when we get older.

It's time to stop waiting at the gate.

Did you ever have a friend or family member ask you for advice on something they thought you were an expert on? Did you try to downplay the "compliment?" Did you feel uncomfortable and "unworthy" to be considered an expert? Instead of worrying about pretending to be someone you're not, recognize you have reached a whole new level on your journey. You might think of yourself as an imposter, but you have as much of a right to be here as the next person.

This feeling doesn't go away as you continue Stepping Forward. Once you've made progress for a period of time, more and more people will see you as someone to reach out to for help and advice. You may feel overwhelmed at first and it might even affect your confidence, something I've always struggled with. Pangs of doubt and fear creep up on me anytime I start a new venture or try to learn something new. I've had more than my fair share of mini panic attacks about this book. It wasn't until I decided to own my expertise that my confidence grew, the quality of my work increased, and I finally overcame my imposter syndrome.

A "UNIVERSAL" EXAMPLE

Andy Weir, the author of the popular science-fiction novel (and now motion picture) *The Martian*, is a full-time software engineer. On the side, Weir wrote short stories and shared them on his barebones blog with only a handful of readers.

In 2009, without anyone's permission, Weir decided he wanted to write a sci-fi novel. After struggling to find a publisher, he published one chapter at a time on his blog, but his readers begged for him to turn it into an eBook. In the span of a few months, *The Martian* sold over 35,000 copies!

A few months later, after garnering the attention he deserved, Weir signed with a book publisher, an audiobook publisher, and sold the movie rights! *The Martian* is an enthralling story, but not perfect. Can I tell Weir self-published this book? Yes. But is it still a good story? Yes. Weir had one goal in mind: entertain the reader. Nothing was going to hold him back. Not even his fear of being somewhere he shouldn't be.

"I'm improving, I think I'm pretty good at coming up with stories and plots. I think my characters tend to be thin. I need more depth. And I think the prose, the actual wordsmithing, is often clumsy. Hopefully, someday I will be actually good at it," said Weir in a recent interview.

We can all learn something from Weir's example. Sure, we might feel like we don't belong, but inserting yourself into these circles can sometimes yield surprising results. Like Weir, I don't have a writing background, but I've forced my way into this tight space and have made a difference. To me, that's all that matters.

LEARN TO OWN IT

I dabble in writing and podcasting. I also have a full-time job as a supply chain analyst. And I'm a new father. I wear many hats, so it is hard to consider myself an expert in any of these facets. But one thing I strive to do is own the different areas of my life.

A few months back, I started a podcast with my friend Justin. I struggled early on with confidence, afraid I didn't know the subject material well. After receiving some negative feedback, I doubted myself and thought, who am I to teach this material?

"Own it," Justin told me, "You don't need to be an expert; you've already lived this stuff."

I failed to realize one simple fact: yes, I am not an expert at anything, but I am good at a lot of things. When I finally stopped worrying about my expertise and instead focused on my life experiences, the podcast sounded a lot better. By owning your work, you convey confidence. Even if you don't have the answer, owning the problem means trusting in yourself to find a solution.

We live in the age of instant knowledge. If we don't know something, we whip out our smartphones and Google it. It's safe to say you can become proficient at anything in one afternoon with a few keyword searches. However, how often in life do we hold back in fear that we aren't good at something? With a new mentality, approaching a venture by owning it will lead a much more confident you. Imposter Syndrome is quivering in his boots just thinking about this new you.

LEARN BY TEACHING

Something that comes easily to you might not for others. When someone seeks out your advice based on the work you've put out, don't shy away from helping them. Use this opportunity to grow. A great way to learn is to teach someone else. By demonstrating your skills and knowledge in a particular subject area, as well as your shortcomings, you will grow tremendously. As you answer new questions, face new problems, and see from new perspectives, you will continue to add to your arsenal of expertise. Don't be afraid to help others even if you feel like you are not equipped to do so. You'll miss an ample opportunity to not only impart knowledge on someone else, but an opportunity to grow.

Remember, we live in the age of knowledge sharing; the Internet is a powerful learning tool! My go-to response when I admit not knowing something is, "I don't know, but I can find out." In college, I didn't go to study marketing, writing, or entrepreneurship, but here I am writing and selling a book all from the information provided to me by the internet. If you ever feel lost or confused along your journey, dedicate some time to learning. For this book, I read hundreds of articles on self-publishing, enrolled in an online Kindle publishing course, and sought the help of other thought leaders. Thanks to the nearly-free information and the help of others, I can now call myself a published author.

STOP SAYING "I'M NOT AN EXPERT"
Lisa never backed down from the *Southern Weddings* job opening because she was a recent college grad with little magazine experience. Alex didn't give up on his startup because he didn't know how to code. Jordan didn't remain in Ohio because he didn't know anyone in Nashville. These Millennials chased their dream with confidence, never apologizing for who they weren't, never admitting they weren't the best candidate, entrepreneur, or musician to follow their dream.

If you aren't an expert, so what? You are in control of your destiny, not the gatekeepers, not the degree on your wall, not your upbringing, only you. Don't apologize for being you. If you encounter a situation where you don't feel equipped to tackle it, don't say, "I'm not an expert." It's admirable to admit you cannot solve the problem right now as long as you can promise to deliver a solution later. Now you turned a negative situation into a potential learning experience.

You don't have to be an expert to keep Stepping Forward, you only need to own it and be more confident in your work. However, how does one measure progress on a life-long journey? In the next and final section, you will learn how to measure gratitude to benchmark your growth.

REFLECTION QUESTIONS:

1. What area of your life do you feel you are overstepping your expertise and feeling the effects of Imposter Syndrome?

2. Would you rather "fake it until you make it" or admit your shortcomings but promise results once you obtain the necessary skills?

3. How can you apply the "own it" mentality today?

3.3 GROWTH AND GRATITUDE

As I write this final section of the book and leave you to continue your journey, I'm tempted to provide you with valuable information on growth tracking metrics, goal setting skills, and hacks for you to accelerate to the top. But I won't.

Propositions litter my inbox such as, "Six months to six figures," and, "Earn 10,000 followers in 10 days." Granted, I signed up for all these mailing lists in the hopes of hacking my way to self-employment, but lately, I've been rethinking the remainder of my strategy.

The internet is saturated with hacks. You know what I am talking about, right? Growth hacks, life hacks, game hacks, basically anything to get you from point A to point B with as little effort, stress, or time. In real life, I'm all for finding faster and better ways of doing a job. Obviously, personal growth and seeking to improve oneself is necessary, but constantly looking for hacks leads to an unhealthy mindset and work ethic.

Sometimes slowing down and enjoying the experience is what we need to improve. I subscribe to a lot of successful entrepreneur blogs. I'm a sucker for them. I signed up thinking I might be able to gain an edge to achieve my dream faster and easier. These people are willing to share their methods and insights for success to help me on my journey.

I hope to join the ranks of these people one day. Heck, I'll even share what I learned along the way. But first, let's do a thought experiment. Let's say your dream is similar to mine – breaking away from the nine-to-five and into the world of self-employment. What would happen if tomorrow I had the opportunity to achieve my dream? (Technically I do, I can storm into my manager's office anytime and quit.) Would I have the necessary skills to generate an income? Could I develop a product or service to sell before our savings run out? Probably not. I'm nowhere near ready for self-employment. Instead, I'm willing to be patient, learn as much as I can, and put in the effort before the time is right.

As sexy as they seem, I'm a skeptic of all hacking propositions. I'm sure the people ahead of us genuinely want to help, but they don't know the journey *you* need to take.

Stepping Forward is a long and challenging process. It's nice to have trail markers along the way to help gauge our progress. A lot of us invest wholeheartedly in achieving certain measurable metrics, such as the number of Twitter followers we have, the income we generate, or the number of pages we write. Although I still find metrics necessary, I view my progress differently: bamboo.

Bamboo Shoots

Bamboo is considered the world's fastest growing plant. Some species can grow as fast as 3 feet in a 24-hour span. However, what people fail to realize are the years of "dormancy" preceding a bamboo shooting out of the ground.

When planted, a seed can take upwards of 4 years before any sprout appears. The reason? The plant first grows a solid foundation of roots to support rapid growth. We need to model our personal journeys after bamboo.

Right now we may seem like we are making no progress or not doing enough to chase our dream. Stressed, tired, and beat down, we may feel tempted to hack our way instead. Don't. I'm begging you, be patient. Or as Henry Wadsworth Longfellow once penned:

"The heights by great men reached and kept
Were not attained by sudden flight,
But they, while their companions slept,
Were toiling upward in the night."

Along my personal journey, I've collected a lot of experiences, some good and some bad, met amazing individuals, and have created a decent following in the past year after years of blogging. Every opportunity I've encountered, I've approached with gratitude because the majority of these opportunities wouldn't exist if I didn't Step Up, Step Out and Step Forward.

To make any progress on your journey, you must lay down the roots of gratitude so you can appreciate the success as it comes. Why do you think 80% of retired NFL players go broke in the first three years out of the league? It's because success came too fast for them to handle it properly. The last thing I want you to do is rapidly rise to the top only to fizzle out. The only way to accurately gauge growth is by gratitude.

Benedictine Monk Brother David Steindl-Rast puts it more poetically. He likens gratitude to water filling a bowl: "We all know from experience that moments in which gratitude wells up in our hearts are experienced first as if something were filling up within us, filling with joy.... And then it comes to a point where the heart overflows and we sing...and for that I like a different term."

The "different term" is gratefulness, the moment your bowl overflows with joy, "it starts to make noise, and it sparkles, and it ripples down."

But, in our modern culture, instead of allowing our bowls to overflow with gratefulness, society "comes in and says 'No, no, there's a better model, and there's a newer model, and your neighbor has a bigger one.' And so instead of overflowing, we make the bowl bigger, and bigger, and bigger. And it never overflows."

Your journey is your bowl. Don't make it bigger than it needs to be. Instead, fill it with experiences, creations, people, love, challenges, and life, and allow it to flow over. It may well in fact take you the rest of your life to appreciate this concept. I know I'm still learning to appreciate it, but of all the personal anecdotes, all the testimonies, and all the metaphors, please take away from this book one thing: The Millennial Way is rooted in gratitude. We seek to fill our life with meaning and purpose and learn to approach adversity with the optimistic hope of coming away stronger. Keep Stepping Forward. Stay grateful.

REFLECTION QUESTIONS:
1. If you had the choice to achieve your dream in an instant, would you take it?

2. What have you been most grateful for along your journey?

3. How do you measure growth?

CONCLUSION

In Panera I once saw a man in his late sixties taking a picture of his coffee, which I thought was strange. It was just an average cup of coffee. It was early in the morning. I was grabbing a coffee to go and some oatmeal and quinoa before work. I noticed how he was smiling at his mug of coffee - a mug, not a paper cup, as if he had nowhere to go. Beside the mug sat a newspaper, the funnies section on top covering the rest of the news. I thought to myself, maybe that's not an average cup of coffee, maybe it's his first cup of coffee in retirement. As he sat in his booth without a care in the world, I briskly walked past, out the back entrance, and off to work.

One day, if I'm lucky, I hope to be like the guy I witnessed in Panera with my work completed and life left to savor. But when that time comes, will I look back and be proud of what I did? This thought often haunts me. What is it that we are looking for? Significance? Accolades? Happiness? I know I am not the only Millennial with these thoughts. It drives our entire generation. How do I know? Because it drives every generation. There is an invisible force pushing us toward meaning and significance in our lives.

I've focused my book on Millennials who had clear cut goals of what they wanted to accomplish. However, throughout my writing process, I held in the back of my mind the ever growing number of Millennials who still feel lost. If you are one of these Millennials who have a vague or no idea of their purpose, keep moving forward. Apply the Step Up, Step Out, and Step Forward formula to every exciting venture that may come your way. Life is great when we have the ability to move as far in one direction as we want, and on a whim, turn on our heels for an entirely new direction. However, your purpose will never be revealed by settling for complacency. Do things that challenge you. Find what scares you. Face what you fear the most. We are all destined for some greater purpose, a purpose far beyond money, fame, or prestige.

My biggest hope is that this book helped you to better visualize your journey ahead by outlining the three most important steps anyone can take: Step Up, Step Out, Step Forward. As you continue along your journey, you may find yourself repeating this process over and over again. As new opportunities arrive, you may find yourself Stepping Up over and over again to new challenges after arriving at false summits. Keep moving forward.

For those of you who forgo the comfortable life to chase your dream, you are not alone. There are millions of us struggling with the anxieties of finding the meaning and purpose of our life. But meaning and purpose won't be found sitting still. We have to move forward before finding it. The Millennial generation is poised to make an impactful shift in this world. I know we will leave behind a better planet and example for future generations to come.

You might have already arrived at the conclusion that the Millennial Way of doing things isn't all that difficult. You're right. The three steps boil down to these nine elements:

1. Take inventory of the skills, tools, and infrastructure at your disposal

2. Give yourself permission to dream

3. Overcome the fears holding you back

4. Make a solid plan to chase your dream on the side

5. Manage friction

6. Be vulnerable

7. Focus on the summit but keep an eye on the path

8. Overcome Imposter Syndrome

9. Learn to be gracious for the entire length of your journey

This isn't a list of steps no one has ever tried before. You are capable of doing more than you think. If you are afraid of becoming someone new, that's okay. The moments leading to change are those we fear the most. These big moments stand out because we know what lay on the other side. Once these moments pass, we will never be the same again. On the verge of change, we tremble. On facing the inevitable, we hesitate. We are afraid of who we might become.

Step Up, Step Out, and keep Stepping Forward. Do not fear any longer. You got this!

ACKNOWLEDGEMENTS

This book wouldn't have been possible without the incredible Millennials I was fortunate to interview and get to know on a deeper level. Lisa, Anu, Suyog, Jordan, and Alex, I wish you all continued success on your journeys. Thank you for helping me to Step Up, Step Out, and Step Forward.

I'd like to also thank those who provided feedback and (much needed) advice on this book, especially Todd, Matt, Tim, Beth, Raz, and Emma.

Thanks to my readers who keep me going every week, especially my most dedicated readers: Maria, Darius, Karin, Emily, Leland, Justin, Byron, Jon, Ryan, Sam, Jacob, Jess, Sean, and anyone who's provided me with support and encouragement. You know who you are.

To my mom and dad for the sacrifices they made for me and my little sister.

Finally, this book wouldn't have been possible without the love and support of Erica, my best friend and amazing wife. You inspire me each and every day. Without you I wouldn't be the man I am today. And Henry, who reminds me daily that learning to Step Forward isn't always easy and takes a few bumps and bruises. This crazy adventure began before you were born, buddy, and I hope it never ends.

Notes and Selected Further Readings

Many of the ideas and thoughts in this book originated from my blog, http://millennialtype.com. I publish a new article and a newsletter every week to my readers. You can sign up for my newsletter at http://millennialtype.com/email.

Introduction

Here is the Pew Research Center report I reference about Millennials leaving jobs: http://www.pewsocialtrends.org/files/2010/10/millennials-confident-connected-open-to-change.pdf.

Here is the 2011 study about employee engagement at work: http://www.gallup.com/poll/150383/majority-american-workers-not-engaged-jobs.aspx.

Subsection 1.1

To see what Anu and Suyog are up to, check out their company site at http://driftaway.coffee for more information. Order some coffee while you're at it.

If you are curious to learn more about my film internship, here is a behind-the-scenes video of the film I volunteered on (there might or might not be a picture of me in a pink hat): https://vimeo.com/14769542.

Subsection 1.2

Alex Rawitz wrote a fantastic review of the genesis of his startup, Verbatm, in this *Medium* article: https://medium.com/matter-driven-narrative/verbatm-word-for-word-f7b477c3c942#.19yupwol7.

To learn more about Verbatm, check out their website here: http://www.verbatm.io/.

I highly recommend reading Stephen Pressfield's, *The War of Art*. You can purchase it here on Amazon: http://www.amazon.com/gp/product/B007A4SDCG/ref=dp-kindle-redirect?ie=UTF8&btkr=1.

Subsection 1.3

To learn more about the Pareto Principle, the Wikipedia page is a good place to start: https://en.wikipedia.org/wiki/Pareto_principle.

This section was derived from an earlier blog post on my blog. You can read the original post here: http://millennialtype.com/to-chase-a-dream-or-make-a-living/.

My wife and I had a blog in college called Cooking in College. It's still up and running if you would like to check it out: http://cooking-in-college.com.

Subsection 2.1

My original interview with Lisa Kirk was published on my blog here: http://millennialtype.com/being-prepared-to-chase-your-dream-lisa-kirk/.

If you would like to see some of the work Lisa has done with her personal blog that started her journey, Something Pretty, you can find it here: http://something-pretty.net.

Subsection 2.2

This section was a combination of two different posts on my blog. The original Jordan DePaul interview can be found here: http://millennialtype.com/the-artrepreneur-jordan-depaul/ and the original post about managing friction can be found here: http://millennialtype.com/managing-friction/.

Before Brittany Kennell was made famous for her appearance on NBC's *The Voice,* she visited our house with Jordan for the interview. You can find her audition for the show here: https://www.youtube.com/watch?v=NU3IJV2UrxE.

If you would like to follow Jordan's journey more closely or check out his music, his website can be found here: http://www.jordandepaul.com/.

Subsection 2.3

Invisibilia, the NPR podcast I mention in this section, can be found in most major podcast apps. However, you can check out their website here: http://www.npr.org/podcasts/510307/invisibilia.

Although a children's book, *The Phantom Tollbooth* is a delightful read for any age. I suggest you grab a copy on Amazon and spend an afternoon reading it: http://www.amazon.com/gp/product/B004IK8Q90/ref=dp-kindle-redirect?ie=UTF8&btkr=1.

This section was one of my earliest pieces of writing for this book since it set the tone for my 2015 blog posts. You can find an early version here: http://millennialtype.com/the-not-so-great-expectations/.

Not telling people your goals might actually work out in your favor. Read up on this Michael Hyatt blog post as to why: http://michaelhyatt.com/should-you-keep-your-goals-to-yourself.html.

Here is the full study write-up by Dr. Peter M. Gollwitzer: http://www.psych.nyu.edu/gollwitzer/09_Gollwitzer_Sheeran_S eifert_Michalski_When_Intentions_.pdf.

Subsection 3.1

The "behind-the-scenes" quote at the beginning of this section can be attributed to Steven Furtick, Lead Pastor of Elevation Church in Charlotte, North Carolina.

More information about the *Twilight Zone* episode can be found here:
https://en.wikipedia.org/wiki/Of_Late_I_Think_of_Cliffordville.

This chapter is made up from a few different blog posts from this past year:

http://millennialtype.com/reaching-destination-successful/

http://millennialtype.com/black-box/

http://millennialtype.com/the-difference-between-making-it-and-succeeding/

Subsection 3.2

To learn more about Andy Weir and the story behind *The Martian,* here is the interview I used for the quote in this section: https://www.washingtonpost.com/news/achenblog/wp/2015/05/05/andy-weir-and-his-book-the-martian-may-have-saved-nasa-and-the-entire-space-program/.

Subsection 3.3

This is the Forbes article I reference in this section about football players going broke: http://www.forbes.com/sites/leighsteinberg/2015/02/09/5-reasons-why-80-of-retired-nfl-players-go-broke/#641c95204e36.

The quotes from the Benedictian Monk David Steindl-Rast can be heard here: http://www.onbeing.org/program/david-steindl-rast-anatomy-of-gratitude/8361.

About the Author

Declan is a writer, blogger, and podcaster with a full-time job on the side. He resides in Pittsburgh, Pennsylvania with his wife Erica, son Henry, and two cats, Rory and Cici.

Every week, Declan publishes a new blog post on his blog, http://millennialtype.com. He also sends out a weekly newsletter to his community of readers to empower them to live, create, persevere, and dream. You can sign up for the newsletter here: http://millennialtype.com/email.

If you would like to get in touch with Declan, feel free to contact him via the following methods (sorted in order of preference):

Email: declan@millennialtype.com

Twitter: https://twitter.com/MillennialType

SnapChat: https://www.snapchat.com/add/decl4nw

Facebook: https://www.facebook.com/MillennialType

ONE LAST THING...

If you enjoyed this book or found it useful I'd be grateful if you posted a short review on Amazon. Your support makes a difference and I read all the reviews personally.

If you'd like to leave a review, please follow the link below to the book's page on Amazon: http://amzn.com/B01E4XX6V8

Thanks again for your support!

www.ingramcontent.com/pod-product-compliance
Lightning Source LLC
Chambersburg PA
CBHW060415190526
45169CB00002B/916